WAYSIDE SANG

ALSO BY CECILY NICHOLSON

Triage
From the Poplars

Published by Talonbooks

WAYSIDE SANG

POEMS

CECILY NICHOLSON

TALONBOOKS

Talonbooks
278 East First Avenue, Vancouver, British Columbia, Canada V5T 1A6
talonbooks.com

Talonbooks is located on xʷməθkʷəy̓əm, Sḵwx̱wú7mesh, and səlilwətaʔɬ Lands.

Second printing: 2018

Typeset in Caslon
Printed and bound in Canada on 100% post-consumer recycled paper

Interior and cover design by Typesmith
On the cover: David Garneau, *Interregnum*, 2010
    Oil on canvas, 61 × 45.5 cm. Image courtesy of the artist
Interior: Ambassador Bridge
    Photo courtesy of Flickr user Nic Redhead under (CC BY-SA 2.0)

Talonbooks acknowledges the financial support of the Canada Council for the Arts, the Government of Canada through the Canada Book Fund, and the Province of British Columbia through the British Columbia Arts Council and the Book Publishing Tax Credit.

LIBRARY AND ARCHIVES CANADA CATALOGUING IN PUBLICATION

Nicholson, Cecily, 1974–, author
    Wayside sang : poems / Cecily Nicholson.

ISBN 978-1-77201-182-1 (SOFTCOVER)

    I. TITLE.

PS8627.I2393W39 2017   C811'.6   C2017-905044-3

To my mother, Patricia of the lake,
who left this spring in search of the ocean.

The Expedition is very flexible. It comes right from the problems. Whatever happens, we try and solve the problem by whatever means necessary.

—G. WARREN

How does one replace the image behind the word?

—M. NOURBESE PHILIP

CONTENTS

FOSSIL FUEL PSYCHE

fossil fuel psyche

pressed for   time

means for
transformation
                    means

will travel or   drift

The necessity of trying to represent what we cannot, rather than leading to pessimism or despair must be embraced as the impossibility that conditions our knowledge of the past and animates our desire for a liberated future.

—S. HARTMAN

cash gas pumps itself into a self
in motion self-powered

a time before
there may be a time after

last stops the railroad

muddy places of manufacture
and heavy industry wracked

drawn-back crumbling increments
of ground

measured ground

acute
diminishing aperture grooves

townie, a one car pony class model
mechanic wakens

music for the eco-elegiac
Middlebelt Road bridges to tunnel

come away with me passenger
comfort

corrugated ground has laid out
tongues
            of rigid structure
            in a fledgling industry

investment snarls
bundles   of spruce
                ash and cotton

to lift and to move   forward
reliable control of   success
                        formulas

every white relation
        this neck of the woods
related to ford the motor co.

run through my point of view
liberation seceded

formally withdrawn far from
diluted milk gruel

coming up here to ends
of roads a factory from fields

truck-trailer model efficiency containers

delivery at the speed of electricity

a new world drives
the universal car a cat among ponies

hot one marriage of style and power

style meets utility
as machines become art at fair pavilions

demonstrations, landscapes built for cars

the great multitude communicates
without wires things tend to rattle apart

puncture-proof tires on the shoulder

conjuring something new in verges
a right-of-way

trailing proof: rubber glass the past shrapnel

break-even roads rail intermodal waterways
inland trails and paths

where wagon roads' single-
minded con-
              quest of spur line and through
lines
convoy for
                      mutual protection mired
                          in meaning
stall livery horses power
finning fly-
wheel
        and vanadium steel then

as now   durable tires
                             key to victory

to any race through the Bonneville salt flats

in a pleistocene lake basin
in retreat of continental ice sheets

modern is toolmaking land-speed records

through traditions of settled pots and pans

is fine knives,
tomahawks, fowling pieces

semi-automatic action of factory long arms

early repeating arms won't take the bail out

just auctioned everything off
right down to the bare logo

automobile production the yardstick

myth of carbon-growth incentives to be deployed

low crude prices continue to take their toll
and we continue to live

as the gold price peaks foster ill opportunities
for too many players in every sector

more drills out all year round declining
a turning point in dependency ratios

the gold scene drills into numbers'
steady increase

a finance *sic* shit ability
to renew the lines, morph and misprice

contaminating groundwater surfaces, wells

composite loss trend borders tracks trail
commodity reports to war population centres

rebar, bared bones in spalling infrastructure
tone as places in ongoing crises of water

delirious – it's all this or nothing – fatigue

melts of semicoherent poetry homes
puttering things to do

things to do once there is a timeless day
of almost pure concentration

to unpluck neural machinery from bone spurs
curling spine, driven C-shaped

matters of spine decompress blowing past
inhalants conduit particles ultra-fine particles

corpuscular rays
alight

throngs of tracks

five cars beside the
tender

new high-speeds

four-lane and turnpike
future

look bright in-

deed time you'd work
to buy

a car romance
road = life

call of the open

the blights of lodging
road objects

market get-away
standards

navigation for
vagabonds

camp edges broken-down
bevel burrs

useful
ornamental differences

master and apprentice

machinists have an aura
about them

a north american system

clocks mechanize time

synchronizing
spokes driven into hubs

mettle pushes
inky type to paper press

grown hermitage of thrushes banded

to a flutter of juncos
                              at the end of the year

we had nothing
we had nothing but grasshoppers

for Abner Jay
a real cultural attraction

vintage postmodern strip malls   ubiquity

mutation
modes of surveillance   fields lightly snowed

wonder about the roads investment overwhelmed

the marvel of small-scale agriculture and manufacture

everything of displaced once dispossessed
workers

collapse of agriculture
once there was no way to stay in food

independently, no way to care for home
self-sufficiently

of people once horded and racked
once holded and trapped
once darker I was

an influx of rural working-class migrants
employed in extraction construction transportation

mines and factories, mechanics and domestics
waiters, porters, and clerks, still in these industries

tourist to you now, roucou

ska rock-steady granddad walks became motorways

ROAD SHOULDERS

road shoulders

verges   *interrupt progress*

wander into the ditches
      form a breach

the picture plane interval in transit-space

                 heaping dirt
        onto the edges of a wildfire

smoulder on the verge, taking up trees

The rushing horizontal band becomes a shape, and then, when you step into it, a form. Time slows.

—D. GARNEAU

where things were found ourselves those days   stretched
across a bond

semi-trailer black with burgundy flame detail   all out

everyday felt to two cans of coke and a mickey of rye
strings of substance pull through black holes
                                        for home
so long mould the damp sprung

there was no controlling the heat or the bedbug
                                flashbacks

shared laundry and all the domestic tasks made public

hit the road
hove time
                                        discipline to muscle
won't have to drive too far
just 'cross the border and into the city

wherever
the final destination takes this it'll be   higher ground

years that slide by rode out kept her head down
or held high
                        when to fight and when to move
junky and dusty
desegregate

every-which-way plaits

what was going to happen anyway
              who got tortured in the process
                                    crossfire
stories
when the reception is good channel

the rest
left behind bold frequencies

rays and disc fuse common chicory blues

trampled transplanted cultivated
from wild for a wilds

amiss some straight hours drive shoulder
to shoulder lids languid
a close pass
that last 4-×-2 set of wheels

throws up dust
rubble cloud forms of alarm

ache awake   *I got the will to drive myself sleepless*

custom not customs got to or gotten through

land lifts the road
rises to meet

where you are at
passenger

how did you come to be
so out of reach

in just a few years

well I remember well

those lips
a seal of callous

on a mouth thin-seeming
till the bottom one
plumps out

how did you get to be so free
and far

from hand-coursed thigh
in Hopper summer light

power lines held by birds
of prey the hostile expanse above

ditches teeming floral invasive
wayside fleurs

late summer the shoulder sang

holds breeze by
the course of the drive

ravelling winds furl sparse treetops

semi-trailers startle traffic to attention
righted to the middle steady

a point of calm

a sense of pedal to headrest
never lost hope of going somewhere

a waiting trench the front across the dash
deep open road through the window

on the glass
bokeh crystals of settlement

streaming past mirror side appears larger

after all the lakes hold ashes and fur

long route tapers to a blue-strip august

the walk along here I was a daughter then
along a highway

on the route she shines on
leaning into the path as nettle heavy with rain

hard to the city 101 rock, concrete drillers
horns, bips, garbage trucks' backup brakes
hollowed-out mufflers, shouters, static groups

humming your process lists and schedule
talk out loud calculating with brackets

sang out loud looks like you're talking
to yourself again

forget about keeping it sound to a body
tensed, ready to strike

sirens, there's a study in sirens

ready to move
that motherfucker reluctant to pull over

who hasn't ever had to call first responders
to an "underserved community"

for his mum or for someone else's love
you just met them face down at the bus stop

course arteries urban renewal drives removal

there are times that a car bends perspective
in its motion
                    making room

measurable extents some kind of care
comfortable-enough front seat

shelter

capacious hearts attend to traumas

there are times
        startled by the good of nature

windows down
        cause a pressure drop, oh pressure

let the real sun in and that whistle of cold air

a day full of making good time

streams the surf-waving tall-grass shoulder

day dreams and muscle memory
some twists comb smooth

from Lakeshore onto Buxton

dragonfly against the window
unexpected flesh

awake rain-spotted
northern towns to your southern ones

truck-stop tourist-shop friends
who'd be good to know
come emergencies

never breaking ground

trace feathers
kept bones to burn for ashes to disperse

drawn out by the *unreal estate* of ditches
taxed into being

fields razed then cultivated grid sections
disregarding rivers
                              and migratory routes

skim the foundation of glacial sand
silt and gravel bites into Erie

built-over grounds
of rcmp-burned homes

the Caldwell members as with the Qayqayt
sans registered land base

at the junction of foot- and flyways
five-lined skink and the fox snake

mud and the musician – mechanic drives on

crises of carceral logics
uncontained and homeless

where the tongue is tied
is tender

I remember I forgot
I had difficulty with talk

while skin carries forth
while my cotton and corn

mind of a picker

have I lost
lifted and moving
in multiple moments

above all we have lost

a periodic impulse
a pendulum

escapement to movements

the audacity of the hardly slept
escapement out windows
watching hours

caught rides late to peripheries
of bigger towns

London to Kitchener

a truck-stop missus
game of kisses came of wishes

it pours we poured *chasing waterfalls*

never could own the wild lilacs
regal thistle clover and tall grasses

long strand sinew her copper
carries on through it all

red-breasted whirs top the meadow

bed down on found paths
to concrete quarries off a sideroad

flowers bloom who loves   a bloom
delible

meadow   reminds me of a puzzle
          captivated us hours over days
wildflowers
                    like blue ridge mountains
hard to piece back together

caught a slip at the gas station a new ride
in a new direction
                         the language
in memory of winding carolinas far gone

bits rags frag embittered
bloom
          was an orange glow of city light
pollution

against the sky cast cosmic pulses
you remember the first time you saw this

once more had to getaway getting late
life grows later sorting

won't be around this old town anymore
for a long long time

well to be under stars bless
a moon orbit moves

with time
less and less its echo in the rift

crunch stripwhite stripewhite stripes
drone by to somewhere

for the end of that long white line

reminds you of your hands
on the wheel gravel back steep trails

from outskirts to inroads
from a country place to high ground

high ground-protected water supplies
worth the long drive, so much to say

your newborn
bless your life, honey, the stars

fallin just like rain that night

breathed hard she arrived

from a farm to and from a country
school, the bus

forty-five minutes both ways

accented us tied to mast painted
                    mangroves and storms

leaned in in such a way
that even now our backs are still in it

PORT OF ENTRY

port of entry between states

altered
        under and over water

solidity of form

        best achieved by the light
          falling against it

in some dramatic and productive way
light returns and falls against us

I saw then very clearly that a border is neither a line nor a long tall fence, but a waiting room. It's a waiting room with a pin-up calendar on the wall, it smells with glue and the wood of cheap pencils. There people are stripped of everything except for the meat that can sit and stand upon request.

—V. MORT

there's good work at chrysler and the canadian border services agency

nubs of trees by the river carrying a border that iced over

this winter they were as blue bridge transport trucks passing

through slim residential/retail streets, odd houses in the wind tattered

tyvek apparates construction   angels
vacant homes and the still-to-be-built   become common here
and here it seems *occupy* has purchase   as necessity has purchase

too cold lots hard on the birds never took purchase

unbearably local and temporal the need for humanizing round

the lakes *create a physical statement*   *whether a painting or a drum beat* data tunnels a bridge of ancestry

logic of borderlands
against the myth of hybrid

low tire on one side
constantly pulls in this direction

herds of failing motors

the fix-in-mud-type white-speaking
ensures a port of entry

to "enter" land

pedestrians risk the miles longer on foot
and buses grey as the trains gouge

borders determine sovereign privileges
the thirsty archives at sea

canna lily medicine and ornament
for use on a journey

walk is a march through frostbiting

paint under sticky licks of amber finish

hard routes on a faint back-axle suspension
suspicions

feel the gear teeth chipped stripped designated

      waiting in rooms face repeat questions
      about having ever been arrested

the system could be ground down
a way over time

if not the car is lost

smatter of skills, smoke and gears
alas, it's your transmission

      ever been placed in handcuffs
      ever charged

as though what's legal matters

matter restores refusal. will returns tomorrow

fleeting through border again black in the belly
meadow marsh to a march of pavement

inhalants exhausted is more particulates
particles and ultra-fine particles
all kinds of dust

shred of tire
simple flags seem mines or pipes

ditch lines of minor valleys
discarded clothing looks to still hold life

as with plastic or glass
flung containers out containers of volition

pylons pink-red cracked faded plastic
dans cette voie guardrails garbage clouds

weather roadblock paths severed by fallen tree
branches

another accident, cars backed up before detours

from somewhere along a path
between the marsh of a ditch
and a railway esker

heading north
through territories of walkers

from the ditch-side window
nothing like the mountain
causeway

if you are a lake south
like I am a lake north

underground as far as Jackson

Chatham past the lake
steps learn and remember

incoming atmospheric
rivers atmosphere old currents

lighten up that migrant narrative gears to war

ministerial authority in the immigration system

nipping and eager air of southern senses
north americas institute reform, claims plummet

continents not been designated
to each year a basin sews well-founded fear

reasons trauma in a 400-square-foot office
everyone cries

come to know roles and when to realize them

to be trusted to protocols to net to sync
fine community slipstream

machinery sucks us in – relays our lines into scales

yet the work resists knowing

unseen labourers
everywhere everyday pick in the shade
                    of mountains

beginning-to-end grit lasts
fresh commodity

mouthful of water – a liquid gem

lead in the blood of your children

may we all
feathers incline in planes side by signal

trust the bass led to funk made time
dance

        found pocket of black light climb

rustling swish the drawn-out
talks confiding

swifts engineered for sky
aerial weather

long months the wings beat
as oars put in

take air and run the holes
rarely taken to ground

evade systems enfolding
highways and canals

patrols scale surveillance
transmute radio

cyberscope handles
manually input resurge signals

intimate feel of brakes
used too much

squeal worn insensitive
unresponsive

indicators or indications

trauma takes more time

bodies through climates
rolling stone

sharp shoulders

ponding forms potholes
leaching

rainbows of oil solvents
in washouts

burst sunforged visions

coal
a mountaintop removed

caravan
saharan highway to the sea

carved into concrete
borders

zoos to prisons

those dear in cages
under the library

borders' better sides

beneath hospital
and holding cell windows

wings trapped in amber
headstones

far from shiny condo

tracks contaminated

under
ground water habits

great lakes' deep sense of time
studded with isles
a basin

river to sea
stable shoreline fretwork

mangrove root system
staves erosion

became here – on this edge
listening to

spotless mother plates giving song
singing *hey baby, it's your time now*

ready and the music shores up
banks

risen

chorusing
hours once again ready to move

feet blistering failures keep leaving the ground

now we know
each other's easy laughter

roll down the window for air

the hay is tall

we've been surviving the assay
together cordage-rigged enterprise

again in a truck passing by fields
and workers

refuse erasure
in defence of land – precious bodies

going to sleep, a light sleep
listening for the phone

arrest intake forms on the bedside table

WAYSTATIONS

waystations
destination a performance

hotels with bars spill out
                      into parades
and fests
           in the street festival-staid

expanses fray by fray with a future

Infrastructure is not only a vehicle of domination and violence. It is also a means of transformation. Alternative worlds require alternative infrastructures, systems that allow for sustenance and reproduction.

—D. COWEN

frisson gliss sparks brick   the mood
or signature colours   in our palette

render same and bring
a candle and a cup to outdoor vigils –

shoulder to shoulder   discordant culture
bends notes   each lot, phenomena
purpose with simple ratios   the moon

one-to-one study   up from balconies
backyards fields

                                                a window
in the ground, even, dignified   still warm

face up
by a rake of coals as late forms

a sleepy eyelid   waxing moon
venus low compliment   on the horizon

scattered coals of some madly formed city
burning

heaps clock past the precipice
grills on cop cars

days baroque at the pyre heart *fire*
not kindling we agree something is different

green light, zimbabwean flag
pause
        in Hamtramck green
Mbare Township tertiary
green-yellow

haven't seen any birds yet
                    this visit

and I've been looking

for rides at the station
come by ways

drainage grates' steam cycles
ankles

groups shout then disappear
although

many appear *aggressive and ready
to fight* to be listening

pub-dub bassist sound
pool-table green

"he lives in a bad house,"
she says to her gal by the sink

the stall doors won't close
unless you hold them

while holding space
as it collapses try to relax, *hey*

come back when it's summer

at the diner dressed up

end of pavement days in sun
black fades to grey

dining conditions curtain-yellow
after all the strip fades

breaching conditions

refuse to cry eyelid pinch
food service open late

leaned on the counter laid claims
to her face

a quiet intersection after hours

where dimly lit desire
paths of coyotes form a late run

motor city a misnomer
with the uncovery
of velodromes

free the water

climbers
mark the metro tower
raised up and whitewashed

hours north
water nonpotable

land travelled on foot
raising childs

water is life

crofters and fishers
invasive

about this lake

love running the course
heading north again to lane

Tri-Cities through the Sound to the Sault

all thoroughfare passing you by
when you park catches up

quiet has a home
unrustled save the wind

whisper hair
flaps

the laundry hung outside

how to remember family

spoke dark early
surfaces burning to the touch

slices in frequency
lush and metallic aerosols of ozone

at a rest-stop monument
to sacred erratics

a storm came through
mustard flowers

in green brassica oil seed

genetics grown
wild along roadsides

escaped fields to ditches
through schoolyards and parks

plants plowed back into soil

come back to me
as the way dives by dry lakes

150 miles to the next gas station
60 miles to the next church

bound to foothills of the rockies

Bluebird Motel
paradise on the prairies

taking the long way
atop the ripple and buckle shift

torn buckle crust-carved surface

like core-bleeding volcanoes
the blacktop amplifies heat

durational, is visible at night

all the roads come through beats
of fibrous hearts

lace of navigable tracks
a spatial syntax legible from space

unknown years on the road a part
movement wheels will

rest is in the distance
while passing motels given over

to early breakfast
breaks in the four, fives, or sixes

washing hair in the truck stop
decent bathroom sink

fair moment smoking
under a sweet knot of trees

still standing despite manifold
exhaust-rolling fevers stretched

SONGS ALONGSIDE

brothers, pragmatic gearheads
– songs alongside

cordage workers

colour retting in open air
methods that unify bast fibre

big tires
displacement V8's
chrome wheel dual exhaust

action of poses acculturates
beauty

racing stripes
built movement between forms

Barreling like gut born love songs / Your ancestors
are smiling / As we pass the time / When we ride /
It's language

—T. EISEN-MARTIN

that last *telephone to heaven*
on the block

shoes discarded, the mismatched
pair conspire in small talk

uncle buffers the rural
list lost in thought reef

hears the mosquito-bite-sting
sounds at night on a wait

late still a cutter – editor busy

sits by a fan propping open
this paint-peeled window

listening to a neighbourhood

The Entertainer eerie chimes ice cream

fireflies that pulse

fireworks well after the holiday

pinch of rubber on pavement
distant airplane

it's a real ritz
loft-cheap boulevard

under a harvest moon
set in ribs of clouds

underground resistance
takes the front stoop

got a car, so is grown

summer now falling away
late pedal steel gives an ambient hum

mechanic – griot left home following emancipation

mobility quests to travel truth-telling

to audiences present dependent on earning dollars
at a local factory – institution

form the front row to the main set medicine show shine

ancestor cousins elemental voices land-carrying

signals bone-dry tired of being wearied

knuckles blued rock emerges past a mania

downhearted blues smite born free until the last breath

crossing lengths for generations
necessarily

                                                        north
to reach in some ways a more secure

non-belonging

siped for winter, pumped tires
airs of remaking reroute

at the end
of a person begins   a recount

what could have been
                                   given or said

what is lost
comes in clouds of exhaust

                                dust in cattail fluff
a bundle of rags worn too dirty to be clothes

return to work the art was never meant for

side of the road
broken-down vehicles

retooling next-generation
precision

slitter services
pose a multiyear downturn

buyouts to white-collar admin

at-least-you-can-deal-with-it-sooner
industry under stress

gives a light-vehicle forecast
production schedule shift

wheel stolen? we can help
we'll work with ALL insurance

against a nostalgic glow
pending plant closures

as automakers downshift

the proposition of new
manufacture

once again record profits
herald a decline
in workforce lineups

Lansing
Detroit/Hamtramck
assembly

flattening sales
cratering interest in sedans

balance sheets for profit
axe production shifts
and kill models

free press
rebuke lists shift reductions

in defiance, numbers and respectability
respected in the numbers trill
luminary

document
a dream book air of remaking

lanes open for the fray small town
golden towers

                    hoisting the tiger network
                sounding thousands of crossing

the AM band over to FM
99.5 on the dial radio crowding bodies

child of that microbial response to loss
as resistance says little

listening in to fragile
rooftop islands in the coastal spillage

eight-lane slivers rush hour on the Michigan-10 to the embassy
for 8 a.m. sun came up like the freeway had burst an artery
just outside of Dearborn

youngest of Tosh's sons stood in line for a permit
travelling the same border moment as late nineties Black Uhuru

made plans for Chicago later that summer, which never

and decades later I read an arrest for medicine made

unable to speak or move with intent
part of my brother, part of my sister   family hangs pictures

heading *home* with Mavis, Little Willie John, and Ann at the window slow drops beat the wipers

wayside singing highway seven

north of sweet grass

a slow leak in the tire

still on to black diamond

eventually Drumheller

to visit a brother linear
scatter in thousands

of distinctive foothills
erratic train late till

amid the highly fractured

and other landslide debris

      neither
broke-up nor rounded-down

almost unmarked and whole
despite the biting striations

as it were – carried on top
or in the upper part

of megalith pulses
of cold climate moving
as it moved – thick-bedded

micaceous feldspathic light
arisen from transformation

grey-pink to purplish
in the heat and pressure

fissures of frost action
otherwise unweathered

DAUGHTER, IMAGINE HER

daughter, imagine her
closed ends and other not

all the wiles
and beauty outcomes

a bloom and a plan
stir the upper atmosphere

running a brisk breath manifest
of a changing state
cloud

particles in the chilly air
streaming scarves, a light wool

The narrator's father will never truly know a free and sovereign life, having had not just his country but also his imagination invaded.

—E. DANTICAT

stopping at every cart
corners

belong to aunties

through inroads
they brought you
to the centre of town
them down with your visit

mother was a turtle
baby brother named obeah

journey's end abides

       ruminates
       until mama day
       light crept under the door

ends to the going, an arrival to return

beauty an aftermath, a bloom conceived
in october '73

born in a bear market
day after Nixon resigned

price-setting mechanisms galloped
the Tigers lost to the Rangers

Eddie Nalon
bled to death in the segregation unit
at Millhaven, in Bath, Ontario

my birth day is a day to remember
unnatural deaths inside

what was held down we will lift up

under way one month alive
withdrawn, apprehended/relinquished

to a fifteen-year bloom of flames
blowers and speed

economy since
has bread
                    worse words than *stagflation*

indexes bottom out to country summers

it was a framed print in the house I grew up in –
Alex Colville's *Horse and Train*

there once were as many horses as people

millions of pounds of shit were shovelled daily

horses walking in giant wheels

once every motor was a horse

horses whose job it was to walk in a circle

horses who did everything

horse flu shut down the economy
more than sixty per cent of them died

imagine sixty per cent of our engines
stopping right now and fewer than half of them starting again

growing up we always had a pack of dogs, usually four
held in prestige among many familiars
them and a few cats we let indoors
though we loved every bird, mouse, tadpole, crayfish
froze in a spring frost we grew more conscious of weather
wide skies read power lines hum dove coos
the leaves turnt dirt melt change on the breeze creaks
and rain the gravel trucks of spring full by slow
then empties in summer barrelling too fast past our hillbilly stake
mother threw potatoes later hard to explain
to the police who got called in from a county over
drove out to say, "ma'am, you can't throw potatoes at trucks"
then all polite as we stood with our pack and stuck to our guns

good scent of gasoline barrel in the barn era
the distribution of labour spiders and must
hay trouble lifting bales except straw wood
picked rocks currants weeds vegetables berries
chewed all summer on comfrey
hungry dreams of ice cream
and brown kids special someday
hanging out after school
at the donut shop smoking or working
at school as much as possible
and on lunch hours learning extra
down with the av kids shop and drama
or running track pitching backstops
wishing behind trees running everywhere
creaks staid knees and the odd knuckle
some doc visiting said I was growing
full height ache at thirteen gangly
like a horse could be when they said wiry
because of wires I suppose the episode
under the steel moon on top of blue snow
barefoot that drive to break free inexplicable
homing soars over property lines and fences
that chestnut mare skipped across ditches like
she knew we could only hope to board her, just
escaped at night no doubt she actually flew home

here because I'm here on a thread

I hear threads backed up to a wall of sound
with wheels

and this little room
to breathe in is driving the exhales

thrust to gallery

discourses
of era law policy papers acts

pains absent in
liberatory TV on the Radio

          smoke
watch them fall   them all an intellect
      of collisions well-anticipated

it's not a way to think all the time

passenger with or I was
driver dream / didn't dream

home, going-home thoughts
when they're useless

billow
over cousin fields of winter

great lake shores cut the sole
shell pieces in undertow

joy drifted over glorious – the banks
snowy risk

imagine her equable

in current industry
hard labour or cumulus clouds

with will
a well feeling, love as a state of many

scarce combed through ease some evenings
gain control of time and I work

I work for nobody – nobody's spur road
spread copper gold tiger rocks rust
valleys of emotional commodities
linked in a jumpy price

no rush cracks the cairn case
lines of scarification

free burns build on down here
where touch has been lost guns atop
tipples – industry's legacy: the police state

wrists wash the window on the high hat
quest – no adjectives, just: enter, fight, exit

hulks, decommissioned warships

anchored in mud, sediment

washed-up lattice habitat

shores, coast, or on the banks of

Susquehanna – older than

mountain ridges it dissects

from orogeny uplift

events when, as part of gond-

wana, the continent slammed

into the turtle – rivers

established in the flat plains

some millions of years ago –

so we stood on the steps of

the municipal art gallery

again facing west, before

the monument at Tompkins

Square and before the totem

pole in Oppenheimer Park –

present *with no feet* things on

maps of single place things

starred project points array

polygons build the hurry

fairly complicating the map-

ping systems with simple-

use case care and caring on

I can never find the right

words for us – a sip of cool

sweet water from the cup of

my palms under pressure the

hereafter is a hustle

crow knows the word *crow*

bird wings trapped in amber

will hear me out free origins –

only high-fidelity

recordings come from paper

too delicate to play back

through the player its rolling

fingers darting – en plein air

place a muss of trouble in

trickles, multiples, sinews

where are you going where

our kind, fulfillment, promise

vigilant light terms, austere

thrives against reaching venery

that tries to touch the hair

all the hammers you had to hammer your head
with projects change you forever

to "bury another acorn" you'll never see grow

then again, to see it grow
rekindling

having taken some decades
the return to this new wave

how a new wave is being talked about now that
there isn't another forty years

of space held on the road – auto-memory-glamour
so easy a gift to a hollowed-out space of daughter

say you knew of her – say you knew the day
she was born and that she, they-all, was healthy

as the growled song lines lift in general
not a sound like it was her haves
it was a sound of just so many

say you contributed

this next song of great social and political import

all the textbook declines in infrastructure
edges clung to and alongside making it. make this

mine here, a multiplicity cold and tight

watch for people dear sent down a corridor
Cass movements make shinola

where from all the frontlines
life in light of me

days that stay memory –
accidents,
anniversaries
of assaults,
court,
suicides,
overdoses,
deaths,
clean

your daughter's birthday –

carbon as sticky bumpy molecules form on us

the day we struck out on the road future-deep

beat knows how to take a punch

knuckles have come to hurt to give

small bones
in the hand sting unpleasantly

burns, prickling, the blood rising heat
while there's cooling in the core
narrow as the eyes cat

spine rights and the bristles heckle

bruises fluid in coil – might well resist further damage

the universe and phenomena
have physical causes not spiritual ones

they are knowable
they are knowable   *fucking snipers on the roof*

                physical and metaphysical dignity

he'd been shot while walking,
then crawling
                        alerts cut to the primacy

animalium our bodies massive and unexpected
            astral strength post-trauma

works hard for a living

microtears of tissue build muscle
a bustle of dawn
                        the changing light on faces

flow push back time reeling in this here the backlashes

ward, jar, carceral and national contaminates water-writing
my sleep cedar and pine routes are rock slide water trickles

at a time dirt banks stabilize
meander and erode less and less

there are more and more pools and riffles following wolves

sure. we are the river's course elevating aspen to a flush of thistle

fabric put to use nice and slow as pitch drop tech embers
nestled out canoe and spoons

in/of "this sounded animateriality"

across my chest southbound fibres wander
lines of code training

para arborescence tips with orange-red berry shadows cast in frost

drawing from content drives art-making
spirits stop and listen

harried lines the stress lines – sure lines

to a long white line curved expressive
these firm straight lines curve
volumes of other spaces

years fly by still new encounters
nuance and lilt, nod and gesture

at a glance may be this
sang sans relations as is

a turn of phrase kind of spice
literature of origin
                              run through a culvert

mine not mine is ruination

once shade got so deep
the mane tied itself round its curl

lengths tropic-damp and boreal
hell in the streets, *sister*
                                        we want you

                              held against
tourist
                        rose against consumer

every morning starts awake

having moved
often in sleep spanning ages

that nebula over your shoulder ...

forces slip and language links us as we
cluster on down

an elbow flex in curve
revolution stuck in traffic

saturday

boulevard this
this too my town

queens, gals, our cadre

on the move past the horizon of teeth
height restrictions

rivers to some outpost skirts of north Surrey

welcoming a push through density

breathing on out Leq'á:mel,
Katzie, Kwantlen ... S'ólh Téméxw ways

AFTERWORD

In 2013, at the Art Gallery of Windsor, curator Srimoyee Mitra launched a multi-year exhibition and series, *Border Cultures*, that explored what it means to be a border city. She notes, "Borderlands are liminal spaces where new subjectivities and identities can emerge and resist the colonial paradigm while activating vernacular aesthetics within international contemporary art discourse." Formative creative study resonates in Windsor, as embodied for example in Gloria Anzaldua's classic *Borderlands*, which addresses the "pluralistic mode" of linguistic and cultural ways informed by the border, in geographical, but also unmoored, diasporic, and internalized, practices. Yet, a national imagination is not as engaged as the situation warrants. This is to say nothing of all the formal and informal ports of entry into the Canadian state that are being tried, precariously, every day.

Like carceral logics, the notion of the border, as it determines legality or legitimacy, permeates many aspects of our lives. I have no other place and never have on this continent, still I am made to feel "foreign," no greater than in interaction with policing bodies and at border crossings. Through citizenship and other points of access and privilege, however, I have been able to wander. In brief intervals from work, or perhaps carrying my work with me, I have meandered between Southwestern Ontario colonial cities, small towns and hovels, and through the rural where my childhood was. I have returned again and again to the pacific north coast, nearing twenty years now. When I am around the great lakes, often I continue south, crossing the United States–Canada border at Detroit–Windsor many times over the years. I cross in other places, but when I can, this is my port of entry. This is one of the places I reconstruct as a component of my family origins. I mean blood, birth, and black family here, though the echoes of foster, adoptive, and found family continue to be so necessary and relevant.

For *Wayside Sang* I set out to place myself in relation to my birth father's history. A favourite bit of information that I have about him was that he was a travelling musician. It was in thinking on day jobs, however, and the static demands for artists called out on the road, that led me to study the automobile, its industry, roadways, and hospitality, through and beyond the region all my fathers have travelled. In concert I activated childhood memories of rural car culture, gearhead brothers, mosport park camping, and so many escapes out on the road, on foot, as a passenger, and as a driver. These tacks I thought would give way to further study, to consider entwined migrations of black-other diaspora, to locate more of my african descent at this late stage, unmoored and mitigated as it may be. Where I cannot locate my bloodlines, I would honour others' accounts. It seems obvious now that the scope of what I set out to do was in some ways far-reaching.

I have grown more concerned with document and archive, institutional, community, and informal, as my writing practice continues. Bearing in mind scale and history, and desiring not to waste time reinventing any wheels, I feel my individual vantage is limited without research, context, or reference. I strive to be in dialogue as much as I can be present for it. My last book project, *From the Poplars*, had me in information centres, libraries, and archives. These were within walking or transit distance from where I lived and in the same city, province, and country. I did not require academic library cards, subscriptions to journals, or a credit card to access them. It was possible to sustain that study, address queries, and weather the challenges to finish the book within two years. For *Wayside Sang* I did not have enough time and resources to be the kind of researcher and writer some part of me longs to be. There were many barriers to enacting documentary poetics in this moment. The local and pressing concerns in my communities are networked broadly. The people and places I interact with most days have my ear more often than not. These are some of the limits to my capacity to travel.

Research on black migration via specific ports of entry was narrowed in part by constraints to my time and labour. As this effort unfolded, I also grew increasingly compelled by what I would describe as an internal call. Fair to say I became mired in my individual location and in the interest of "how did I get here." When the tide rolls in, if you stand there in the wet sand, eventually you start to sink. It is a pleasant feeling for a time, to grow ankle-deep in these particles of land, even if just briefly, a part of the shifting intertide. The experience becomes unnerving the deeper one settles. Bare feet feel unfamiliar textures. Perhaps you will get stuck. The activation of childhood memories was a substantial and valid part of this work.

While my experience as black diaspora is cherished and clear, it has always been reinforced and undermined by racism and nation-state border logics (and the political economy that informs these). I understand a history of displacement, beginning as a ward of the state. My sense of origin and belonging lacks specificity. It has been mitigated substantially by literary, music, and popular culture, I think necessarily. *Ward* I find to be a difficult word in its connotative and material relation to property, whether national or even carceral – yet, a ward of the state may not be an entirely terrible position. As the years tick by, I have come to terms with non-belonging as being habitat in and of itself, and a not particularly unique one at that.

Listening to the artist Deanna Bowen speak on what is perhaps a lifetime of critical work enacting the archival items of her families' history, "settling a debt to old-timers" and to people who have thrived despite incredible hardship, I am heartened by a sense of familiarity. Not in the history necessarily, or in the stories and memories of someone else's family, but in the realization that I too have come through, must have come through, as we all do somehow, originating in and from multiple places, grounded in movement of resolute peoples. I am a dream and a future, gratefully. I descend in part from musicians. And I was able to locate and situate myself in poetry beginning many years ago. As I look to visual culture in recent years, made earnest and frustrated by my local, I have begun to draw more clues.

Art history, certainly as it represents or involves me, has been suppressed and withheld from many of us, for a lifetime. The contemporary continues to foreground patriarchal, capitalist, and classist value that undermines any righteous sense of creativity. Art, my friend Carmen Papalia reminds me, can be a sensual engagement that need not be dominated by visual learning. Art and poetry, as so many artists attest, can unabashedly take place in community and for people, less for the gallery or an imagined art world. As I feel for texture, for new infrastructure I cannot possibly channel or sculpt on my own, I have found new poems. They too are in concert. Consider Charles Campbell's Transporter Project, begun initially as a visual investigation of the phenomena of forced migration; or Camille Turner's various "sonic walks" which present narratives that explore the complexities of black life in Canada amid a "landscape of forgetting" black history; or Khari McClelland's embrace of music as a "transportation device" uncovering the experiences of fugitive blacks crossing into Canada. We are all concerned with transportation. Even as we dig, build, plant, and root, even as we shelter and grow, we have been, and continue to be, on the move.

For all my reverence and admiration for Detroit as any source of culture or point of origin, I spend time there, and evoke the city here, with humility and restraint. After all these years, I am only ever briefly holed up, for a time there on Cass Ave., these days near Hamtramck, or passing through Dearborn. I am a visitor. I cross paths with writers, musicians, and artists in quiet and caring ways. It is a tough city. I am grateful for the welcome to another place that is not my home – a place where I interact with strangers and acquaintances often friendly at the outset to the likes of me. It is good to be seen. Across the Detroit River is one route for me to trace the origins of my blackness, at a point through which it came to be defined within the Canadian state. How to understand "mixed race" or "multiracial," how significant is the hyphen really, whatever the antecedent, for the hybrid black person with my experience? Uninterested in the privilege of my citizenship, bloodlines, or origin, projections of migrancy prevail – are inscribed on my body – a normative rendering of my phenotype everywhere I have lived in Canada. "Where are you from?" Acts, policies, discourses of assimilation and supremacy designed to restrain the movement of racialized and black people continue today with contemporary displays of policing, education, and care. "Where are you really from?" I owe allegiance to scholarship, art, and organizing that continues to resist this. The routes *Wayside Sang* follows cannot be Canadian as the interlay of territories – Anishinaabe, Haudenosaunee, Attawandaron, Ojibway-Chippewa, Huron-Wendat … – the presence and histories – Indigenous memory as a constant to land, and constitutive to my travels and practice – carry the day. Responsible to this, my citizenship is too much of a privilege for me to hold to being not Canadian, even as the land I occupy is otherwise.

To realize profound mobility and belonging in black aesthetics is to build solidarity unrestrained by borders. I think on what is necessary in the name of water as I come to terms with my own fossil fuel psyche at yet another (ongoing) time of trauma and movement. We will continue to be relevant as networks, communities, and aesthetics gain new qualities. Despite the pressures undermining the worth of my cultural contributions – it took me a very long time to reach this page – courage is amplified as I am embraced. I have learned so much working collectively, in collaboration and rebellion. As I look to the work and community around me, as *Wayside Sang* has formed, let me confirm, this is not a narrative of trauma.

NOTES ON SOURCES

I draw inspiration from a number of sources that have helped form topography, i-mage, history, and a playlist for this book. I reference the music of Black Uhuru, J.J. Cale, Tracy Chapman, Soul Coughing, Abner Jay, Janis Joplin, Scott Joplin, Little Willie John, Ann Peebles, Prince, Nina Simone, Mavis Staples, The Stone Roses, Sturgill Simpson, TLC, Toots & the Maytals, and TV on the Radio.

Some mainstays and filigree I call on with great admiration:

Cowen, Deborah. "Infrastructures of Empire and Resistance." *Verso* (blog), January 25, 2017.

Danticat, Edwidge. *Create Dangerously: The Immigrant Artist at Work.* Princeton and Oxford: Princeton University Press, 2010.

Eisen-Martin, Tongo. "Heaven Is All Goodbyes." In *Heaven Is All Goodbyes*, Pocket Poets Series 61. San Francisco: City Lights, 2017.

Garneau, David. "Roadkill and the Space of the Ditch: An Artist's Meditation." *Overlooking Saskatchewan: Minding the Gap.* Eds. Christine Ramsay and Randal Rogers, 113–148. Regina: University of Regina Press, 2014.

Hartman, Saidiya. "Venus in Two Acts." *Small Axe*, Number 26 (Volume 12, Number 2), 1–14. Durham: Duke University Press. 2008.

Mort, Valzhyna. "Forum: Poets and Borders." *Poetry International* (website), San Diego. February 28, 2017.

Philips, M. NourbeSe. *She Tries Her Tongue, Her Silence Softly Breaks.* Wesleyan University Press, 2015.

Warren, Gwendolyn. "Director's Annual Report." *Field Notes*, 4–9. East Lansing, MI: The Detroit Geographical Expedition and Institute, 1971.

ACKNOWLEDGMENTS

Early drafts of some of these poems first appeared in: *The Elephants*, *Free Roots*, *Poetry Is Dead*, *The Capilano Review*, *Transition*, and *Tripwire: a journal of poetics*, as well as in the *We are not citizens / we are magicians* chapbook (edited by Jordan Scott, Simon Fraser University).

Much appreciation to the Canada Council for the Arts, Grants for Professional Writers: Creative Writing, for supporting this project. What a break.

Thank you to all of the staff at Talonbooks for your patience and support. Charles Simard especially, for copy-editing.

My gratitude to Yaniya Lee for your careful and timely reading and comment on this manuscript. Likewise to Stephen Collis. This book moved so much more fluidly once in conversation with you both.

Glad to have been able to finish a first draft of this book at the Zimbabwe Cultural Centre of Detroit. Thank you to Chido Johnson, and love to all the wonderful folks moving in that midst.

I was fortunate to be the 2017 Ellen and Warren Tallman Writer in Residence for Simon Fraser University, an experience that has contributed to this project. Thanks again to the committee that made that possible.

Thank you to David Garneau for your illumined painting and for the essay I rely on here.

Dearest crew, Mercedes Eng, Ivan Drury, Julie Okot Bitek, Natalie Knight, Hari Alluri, Afuwa, Junie Désil, Nadine Chambers, the Lyonses, the Kytes, and the rest of a poetry community for your invitations and influence, the love and time and laughter, Jordan Abel, Andrea Actis, Marie Annharte, Phanuel Antwi, Neil Brooks, Clint Burnham, David Buuck, David Chariandy, Louis Cabri, Wayde Compton, Christina Cooke, Jeff Derksen, Ayumi Goto, Danielle LaFrance, Tongo Eisen-Martin, Donato Mancini, Ashok Mathur, Fred Moten, Michael Nardone, Jordan Scott, Harsha Walia, Karen Ward, and more.

Much respect and appreciation to those who make Gallery Gachet and Joint Effort possible.

Thank you to my family. To Jeffrey and the salty dog, most of all.

CECILY NICHOLSON is rural, small-town Ontario, via Toronto and South Bend, relocated to the pacific coast now almost two decades. On Musqueam-, Squamish-, and Tsleil-Waututh-occupied lands known as Vancouver, she has worked since 2000 in the downtown eastside neighbourhood, in recent years as administrator of the artist-run centre and mental health resource, Gallery Gachet. A part of the Joint Effort prison abolitionist group and a member of the research ethics board for Emily Carr University of Art and Design, Nicholson was the 2017 Ellen and Warren Tallman Writer in Residence at Simon Fraser University. She is the author of *Triage* and *From the Poplars*, winner of the 2015 Dorothy Livesay Poetry Prize.